LifeThreads Books
Evergreen, CO 80439 www.manifestingbaby.com
ISBN: 978-0-991636-13-6

This book is dedicated to our two beautiful children,
Emma Emaya and Elliott Paul Erik.
Thank you for choosing us.
We will love you to the sun, stars and moon forever.

INTRODUCTION

I wanted my kids to grow up knowing 100% that we all chose to be part of this beautiful love story. I believe our children choose us to be their parents. I could not find any books to tell this magical story, so I decided to create it myself. At this point in human history, there are so many special ways to become parents. This book is appropriate for families choosing adoption at any age, surrogate births, embryo donation, egg donation, IVF, sperm donation and so many other ways families are now magically created. I believe that in every single case, our children were always there. They just waited for a time when we could become healthier and came to us in the perfect way at the perfect time. You can read more about my journey to motherhood in my book Manifesting Baby: The Mother's 30-Day Fertility Journal (www.manifestingbaby.com).

My hope is that this book will help many parents and children easily talk about their love story, whatever that may be. There are two places in the book where you can feel free to share with your kids what you believe and what is age-appropriate for them. Below are some ideas for different family situations.

You Jumped on a Rainbow:

- Later-in-life adoption/foster adoption: God and the angels watched over you every day before you came to us. You were never alone.
- Adoption at any point: She/they (use whatever name or names you use here) slid you down the rainbow safely into our hearts and gave us all the most special gift of our lives.
- Infant adoption: She helped you grow for 9 months and then you were placed into our hearts and arms forever.
- Any situation: This beautiful loving slide delivered you to our hearts. You were watched over every minute (God, angels, or whatever you believe in) until you reached us.
- Egg/embryo/sperm donation: You had many people who helped you slide down this magical rainbow so you could reach us (doctor, donors) and you grew in my tummy.
- Surrogate: You grew inside (name)'s tummy. There was one special person who helped you grow.
- Adoption/foster: Tell anything here about what they went through to get to you (i.e. you jumped on a rainbow, landed in Virginia with your birth family, angels and God watched over you the entire time and after 5 years placed you with us in our hearts). You knew all along we would become your parents. We chose this beautiful path so we could all grow and learn to love.

You Gave Our Family a Beautiful Love Story:

- Say anything more that you want to tell your child here. Whatever you feel is right for your family to add about your family story.

All My Love to You and Your Family,
Shannon R Rios Paulsen MS LMFT
www.manifestingbaby.com
www.healthychildrenofdivorce.com
www.inlovewithme.com

We Asked the Sun:
Please Bring Us a Child

The Sun Said:

Be Patient and Allow Your Child to Grow in Your Heart

We Asked the Stars:
Please Can We Be Parents?

The Stars Said:

Be Patient and Allow Your Child to Grow in Your Heart

We Asked the Moon: Please Can a Child Choose Us?

The Moon Said:

Be Patient and Allow Your Child to Grow in Your Heart

We Had Fun

We Laughed

Then One Beautiful Day

You Looked Down
From the Sky and
Said Magical Words

There They Are:
My Parents

You Knew in YOUR Heart

So You Jumped On a Rainbow

And Slid Right Into Our Hearts

Where You Had Been
Magically Growing

Thank You For Choosing Us.

You Are the Best Gift Ever!

Love Makes Our Family Special

Made in United States
Orlando, FL
18 June 2022

18905583R00015

No matter how your child magically came into your life, it was due to love.
This is a beautiful family love story. We believe in our hearts
that our children chose us. We hope this book helps you tell your children
about your family's special love story and how much you wished for them.

Shannon R Rios Paulsen, MS LMFT is a family therapist and author of four
other books (www.healthychildrenofdivorce.com,
www.manifestingbaby.com, www.inlovewithme.com).
This book was born from her personal motherhood journey. She wrote this
book for her own children and all the other children out there who took a bit
of magic, wishing, and prayer to bring into the world.

ISBN 9780991636136